The 6:42 from London Bridge

Nikki Brown

The 6:42 from London Bridge

DELTA Publishing

You can listen to *The 6:42 from London Bridge* using the free DELTA Augmented app – you'll also find fun interactive activities!

Download the free DELTA Augmented app onto your device	Start picture recognition and scan the **contents page**	Download files and use them now or save them for later

1st edition 1 ⁶ ⁵ ⁴ ³ ² | 2024 23 22 21 20

Delta Publishing, 2019
www.deltapublishing.co.uk

© Ernst Klett Sprachen GmbH, Rotebühlstraße 77, 70178 Stuttgart, 2019

Authors:
Text: Nikki Brown
Annotations and activities: Laura Broadbent

Cover and layout: Andreas Drabarek
Illustrations: Harald Ardeias
Design: Datagroup Int, Timisoara, Romania
Cover picture: Harald Ardeias
Photos: **6** Shutterstock (Lavandaart), New York; **6**, **108** Shutterstock (iconspro), New York; **13** Shutterstock (Undrey), New York; **19** Shutterstock (StockImageFactory.com), New York; **25** Shutterstock (Christian Mueller), New York; **27** Shutterstock (AVN Photo Lab), New York; **30** Shutterstock (Adam Cowell), New York; **34** Shutterstock (Dom J), New York; **42** Shutterstock (Christopher Sharpe), New York; **45** Shutterstock (ParrySuwanitch), New York; **47** Shutterstock (vchal), New York; **69** Shutterstock (Chris Jenner), New York; **104** Shutterstock (Martial Red), New York; **106** Shutterstock (nabiha riahi), New York; **110 / 111** Shutterstock (Bardocz Peter), New York

Printing and binding: Salzland Druck, Staßfurt, Germany

ISBN 978-3-12-501113-7

Contents

Abbreviations

sb   somebody
sl   slang
sth   something

LON
DON

Before you start

1. Have you been to London before? Would you like to go?

2. When you go to a big city, how do you like to travel around?

3. What are the advantages and disadvantages of these ways of travelling around a city?

	👍	👎
🚌		
🚶		
🚲		
🚗		
⛵		
🚆		

4. As you read Raj's story, look at a map of London and try to find out where the places are.

1 A first sign

"Thank you all very much for coming this evening." said the rather large lady in black velvet leggings and a bright green velvet coat which almost reached the floor. "I am sorry you had to wait such a long time, but it's something you are going to have to get very used to ..." She then giggled, paused dramatically for a moment and looked around the room.

"I am afraid that out of the fifty-two of you who came tonight, we can only see two of you again."

Raj looked down at his lap. He was so nervous he thought he would stop breathing. He could feel the girl next to him with the irritating laugh shaking. The boy opposite him, Michael, who had spent the whole evening telling them he was a professional actor already, was still looking very calm. The large velvet lady continued speaking.

17 **velvet** soft thick material used to make curtains and sometimes clothes – 20 **to giggle** to laugh in a silly way – 9 **lap** the upper part of the legs and the knees when a person is sitting – 26 **irritating** annoying

9

"So darlings, it's my job to do the dirty deed. That's what they pay me for. So I won't make you wait any longer. Would number 7 and 33 come and see me over here please? The rest of you can go home."

Raj could not believe it. Number 33. That was him. There must have been some mistake.

He stumbled over to the velvet lady. All around him people were putting their coats on, trying to get out of the room as quickly as possible. It was only when he was standing next to the velvet lady that he realized that Michael was also standing there. He was number 7.

"So, congratulations, Raj and Michael, you have both got a recall. Please be sure to be here at nine o'clock prompt on Saturday morning. And remember to wear loose clothing again. So see you then. And don't forget to practise your Shakespeare monologue. Any questions? No? Well, we'll see you both on Saturday then."

Raj walked down the long stone steps of the Central School of Speech and Drama in silence. He still couldn't believe his luck. He had been chosen to come back again. He had a chance of getting a place at drama school. It was only when he got to the bottom of the stairs that he realized Michael was standing next to him.

"See you anon," Michael called as he disappeared up the road.

"Yes, mm, sure," shouted Raj after him. Was that Shakespeare? He wondered.

As he was walking down Fitzjohn's Avenue towards Swiss Cottage Tube, Raj realized what the recall meant. On Saturday morning, like every Saturday morning, he was supposed to be working in his parents' shop. He would be selling papers, giving out National Lottery tickets and London travel cards.

1 **deed** job that needs to be done – 13 **recall** here: being asked to come back again – 23 **anon** soon (old Shakespearean word) – 30 **London travelcard** ticket which allows travel anywhere in London on trains, tubes and buses after 9.30 in the morning and at weekends

What was he going to tell his parents? Since he was fourteen he had worked in Patel News every Saturday. There would have to be a death in the family for him not to work there. A drama audition would not be a good enough reason not to turn up to work. At least not as far as his family was concerned.

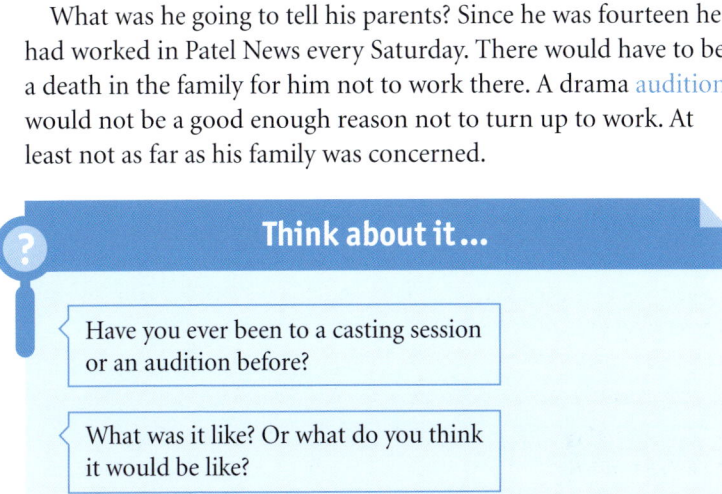

Think about it ...

> Have you ever been to a casting session or an audition before?

> What was it like? Or what do you think it would be like?

---

3 **audition** interview for a role as a singer, dancer or actor

2 What to do

At nine o'clock the next morning, Raj was sitting in a Business Studies lesson. It was a bad morning. Ninety minutes of business studies and he hadn't done his homework.

"Raj, would you like to explain to the class please what is meant by 'the Boom and Bust' years of the eighties?"

Raj tried hard not to yawn. "Sorry, Boom and . . ."

"Bust, Raj, bust. Do try to look a little bit interested. Or have you forgotten everything we did in the last lesson?" Raj could see Neil Young, his tutor, was getting more and more irritated.

"Let me try again. The economic policies of the Thatcher years? Margaret Thatcher? Conservative prime minister for seventeen years?"

Now Neil Young was getting very angry. Raj knew that tone of voice. And he knew he wasn't going to win this discussion.

"Okay, Raj, I realize there is no point in continuing with this. Chloe, perhaps you know the answer?"

20 **Boom and Bust** a time in the 1980s when many people made and lost a lot of money – 24 **irritated** annoyed

Raj sighed. He had no interest in business studies, but had been made to take the subject by his parents.

They wanted him to have a good business head so he would be successful when he took over the shop. The only problem was: he didn't want to run the shop. And he never would. He wanted to be a successful actor like his great uncle, Amrit Kapoor, the Bollywood star.

"Raj, would you like to turn to page 27 in the book like the rest of us?"

Sarah nudged him and pointed with her finger at the page. She whispered under her breath, "Exercises 1a and 2b."

Raj opened his textbook and started reading.

He took out his pen and started to write down the instructions. "So how did it go?" asked Sarah. "We're all dying to know."

"Great. Really great. They want me to come back. There's just one big problem."

"What's that?"

"What am I going to tell my parents?" Raj asked.

Think about it... ?

> Raj is doing business studies because his father wants him to.
>
> Do you think this is right? Did you choose all your subjects at school?

---

1 **to sigh** to breathe out loudly to show pain or sorrow – 7 **Bollywood** the Indian "Hollywood" – 10 **to nudge** to push sb with an elbow to get their attention

3 Break time

Raj and his friends were sitting on a wall outside the College of North West London. It was a friendly but ugly concrete building near Neasden tube station. The traffic screeched past on its way to the North Circular, Wembley and the M1. It was so loud they could hardly hear each other speak.

Neasden wasn't the prettiest part of London but there was a lot to do locally. And the centre of town was only thirty minutes away. For Raj this meant theatre land. For his friends it meant Oxford Street, Virgin Megastore, the Empire cinema in Leicester Square and night clubs like the Ministry of Sound.

"So, come on, Raj. What happened? Have you got a place?" asked Tej as she brushed Sarah's hair. Simon was eating an enormous cheese sandwich as he balanced on the wall. He had just joined them from his English class.

"So, Laurence Olivier. When do you start? 'To be or not to be, that is the question.'" Simon waved his arms around and tried to look serious.

16 **concrete** a grey material used to make a building – 17 **to screech** to scream loudly – 18 **North Circular** road that goes around northern London – 18 **M1** the main motorway from London to the North – 29 **Laurence Olivier** very famous British actor (1907-1989)

"Oh very funny," said Raj. He grabbed Simon's sandwich and took a bite out of it.

"Hey, that was mine."

"Look, I haven't got a place. It's not that easy. But I have got another audition. They call it a recall. I've got to go back again on Saturday morning. I think you have to go several times before you get a place."

"Saturday morning?" Tej looked up.

"Yes, that's the whole problem. My parents don't even know I went to the drama school last night. They hate the idea of me being an actor. As far as they are concerned, I will make Patel News a great success."

"But they know you want to become an ..."

"Sorry?"

A large lorry went past and they couldn't hear a thing.

"They know you want to become an actor."

"Yes, but they think it's just a hobby. And on Saturday morning I've got to be at the drama school when I am supposed to be in the shop."

"So what are you going to do?" Sarah asked sympathetically.

"Tell them." Raj put his head in his hands. "And that won't be easy."

? Think about it ...

Should Raj have to hide his audition from his parents?

How easy is it to be open with your parents about things that are important to you?

---

11 **as far as they are concerned** what interests them – 12 **success** here: sth that will allow you to earn a lot of money – 20 **sympathetically** with understanding

4 Trouble

It was seven-thirty that evening. The shop had been closed for an hour and Raj's father had just come in. Raj's younger sister, Meesha, was doing her homework at the kitchen table. His mother was getting supper ready.

"Lay the table please, Raj. I've got your favourite tonight." She showed him the paratha bread and the dal that was simmering on the stove. Raj smiled weakly. It was not going to be an easy evening.

"Well, it's been a good week, Raj. You know in ten years' time you could have an empire. It could be Patel and Sons. We've sold so many lottery tickets this month. It was the best thing we ever did. And even better – we've had some big orders for fireworks for Divali. You get a good degree in business studies and your future is certain."

Raj carried on putting the plates on the table.

"Did you hear me, son?"

---

21 **paratha** type of fried Indian bread – 21 **dal** a typical Indian dish made of lentils – 21 **to simmer** to cook very slowly on a low heat – 8 **stove** place where saucepans are put to cook food – 24 **empire** large business or organization – 27 **Divali** biggest Hindu festival in October / November: a celebration of light

"Look, Dad," Raj said. "There's something I need to tell you".

He saw his mother's worried look. Even Meesha looked interested for a moment. She sensed trouble.

"Go on, son."

"It's about my future. I need to talk to you."

"Don't worry, Raj. Your future is secure. You just get good A-level results, maybe even go to university and then you can come back ..."

"No, you just don't understand. I want to be an actor. I am going to be an actor ..."

Suddenly his father's face changed. His mother sat down quietly, her head in her hands.

"We've discussed this before. Absolutely not. Acting is not for you. It's a hobby, not a job. No-one becomes an actor in our family."

"But that's not true. What about Uncle Amrit?"

"That was Bollywood. We live in Willesden, Raj, and times have changed," his father went on. "How are you going to support a family as an actor? Just forget it. One day you will realize I was right."

How many times had Raj had this discussion. How many times had he been told to forget it. But this time he couldn't forget it. This time he had a real chance to become an actor.

"No," Raj said, "I won't forget it. I can't. On Saturday morning, I am going to the Central School of Speech and Drama. I have got a second audition for a place at drama school. I have never wanted anything so much in my life."

"You go on Saturday and turn your back on this family and this family will turn its back on you. You don't turn up for work on Saturday and you will never work in the shop again. Then you can work out how you are going to pay for your special place at drama school. You will never earn money at Patel News again."

---

3 **to sense** to notice; to become aware of – 6 **secure** certain – 17 **Willesden** area of northwest London – 31 **to work out** to find out

Raj had never seen his father so angry. But he couldn't stop. He, too, was angry now.

"The money I earn at Patel News wouldn't pay for very much. I've worked there for the past three years every Saturday and all the school holidays for very little money. Minimum Wage? You don't even know what it is."

Raj's mother was sobbing into her hands. Meesha had run off into her bedroom. The dal was bubbling over on the stove and the onion bhajis were burning. Raj realized it had all come out wrong. He also knew he couldn't stay in the house.

"Where are you going?" Raj's father asked, as Raj put on his coat.

"Out. To look for a job."

He slammed the door shut, jumped on his bike and cycled through the streets of Willesden Green.

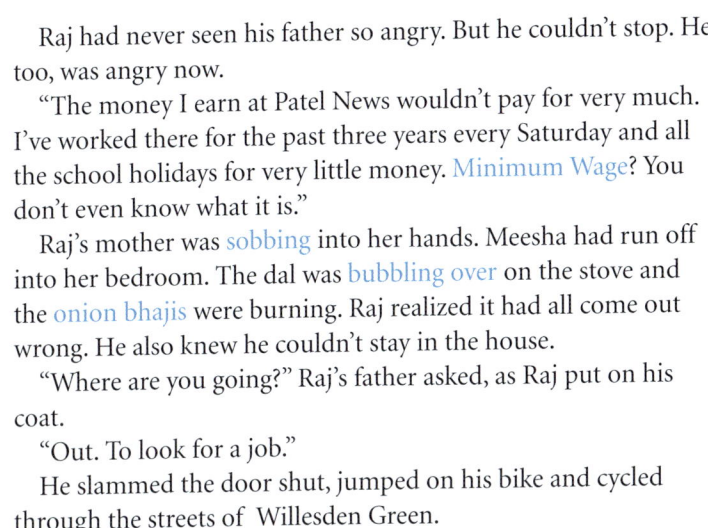

? Think about it...

Do you think Raj's father's reaction is fair?

What do you think the dangers of acting as a career might be?

Is it worth taking the risk?

---

5 **Minimum Wage** the lowest amount of money sb can legally be paid per hour to do a job – 7 **to sob** to cry taking in lots of breaths – 8 **to bubble over** to boil so much that it goes over the top of the pan – 9 **onion bhaji** spicy Indian food made of onion, egg, flour and water

5 A good idea

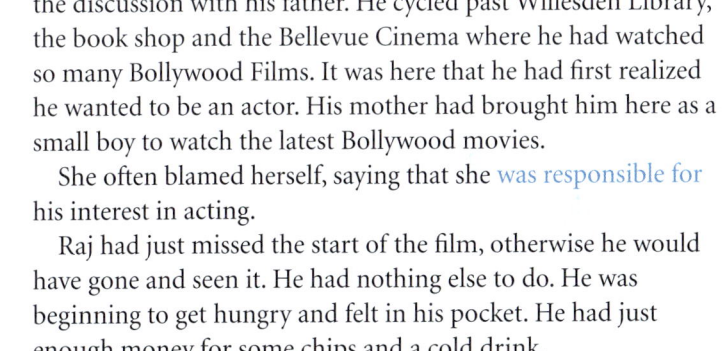

Raj cycled round and round for hours trying to make sense of the discussion with his father. He cycled past Willesden Library, the book shop and the Bellevue Cinema where he had watched so many Bollywood Films. It was here that he had first realized he wanted to be an actor. His mother had brought him here as a small boy to watch the latest Bollywood movies.

She often blamed herself, saying that she was responsible for his interest in acting.

Raj had just missed the start of the film, otherwise he would have gone and seen it. He had nothing else to do. He was beginning to get hungry and felt in his pocket. He had just enough money for some chips and a cold drink.

He decided to go and sit at the top of Roundwood Park. It was where he always went when he couldn't think straight. He put the packet of chips in his pocket and cycled off past the Fire Station, the Jewish cemetery and along Robson Avenue to the park.

---

22 **to be responsible for sth** here: to be to blame for sth – 31 **cemetery** place where dead people are buried

The gates had been shut several hours. They always closed the park when the sun went down. Raj tied his bike up and climbed over the railings. The night sky was lit up. He could see Neasden Temple where his family always went. It looked even more beautiful tonight with its bright red Divali lights.

Raj ate the chips quickly. He had not realized how hungry he was. He licked the paper, tasting the salt and vinegar.

All of a sudden he heard footsteps. The park warden was standing behind him. Now he was in trouble.

"The park's shut. How did you get in?"

"Eh"

"I saw your bike. You know I could call the police. But it doesn't look like you're causing any trouble. What are you doing here on your own anyway?"

The man with a long ponytail sat down on the bench and lit a cigarette. "I often come here to think when I can't sleep. Got girlfriend problems?" he asked.

"No, worse. Family ones."

"Oh I see. You can tell me if you want to."

For some reason, Raj began telling the park warden all about his problems, about the audition on Saturday and the corner shop. It felt good to talk, especially to someone he didn't know.

"You want to get yourself a new job. Then you can do what you like. It's your own life, you know. Whatever anyone says."

Raj was beginning to feel better.

"But what can I do? If I do get a place at drama school, it will cost so much money. I'll never be able to afford it."

"Well ... you could get a job in a restaurant or bar. Or what about getting a job as a bike courier? You've got a bike, haven't you? You can earn lots of money that way. I did once."

Raj's face lit up. Yes, a bike courier. He liked the idea of that.

---

3 **railings** type of fence made of metal sticks – 7 **to taste** to notice the flavour of food –
15 **ponytail** long hair tied back – 27 **to afford sth** to have enough money to pay for sth –
29 **courier** person on a bike, motorbike or in a car who delivers sth for sb

Think about it ...

Raj likes to go to the park to think. Why do you think this is?

Do you have somewhere special you go when you need time for yourself?

6 The Knowledge

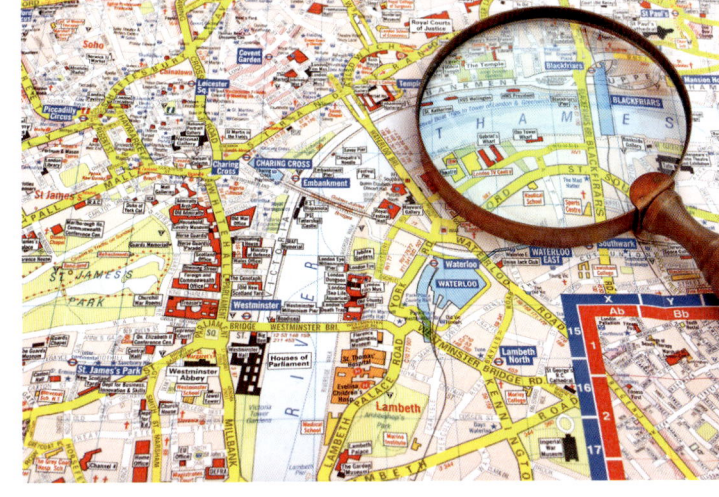

"Love goes toward love as schoolboys from their books,
But love from love, toward school with heavy looks."

Raj stopped and threw himself on the sofa.

"So what do you think," Raj asked. There were only two days to go till the recall at Central School and he was practising his pieces at Sarah's house. Since the argument with his father he had spent most of his time there. Sarah lived alone with her father. He was a taxi driver, who worked nights.

"Do you want the truth?" Sarah asked. Raj nodded. "Well, I think your Shakespeare piece is okay, but you do look a bit serious. He's madly in love. He can't think of anything else. All he wants to do is hold her in his arms. Your Romeo looks like he's waiting for a bus – not his girlfriend."

Sarah saw the look on Raj's face. She realized she had upset him.

---

21 **argument** disagreement; fight – 26 **madly in love** very much in love – 29 **to upset sb** to make sb sad or annoyed

"No, it's not that bad. I mean it's actually very good but, ..."

"No, you're right," Raj said. But secretly he was cross. He knew Sarah was right. He liked her a lot, probably more than he realized and he didn't like feeling stupid in front of her. Or her dad, who had just walked in with a cup of tea.

"What's the point anyway? Even if I get a place at drama school I can't go there. The fees are thousands of pounds a year."

"Well, we all have to start somewhere," Sarah's dad said. "I guess you could always find a Saturday job in a shop?"

Sarah looked cross. "I don't think Raj wants to work in a shop again, does he, Dad?"

"Oh, sorry, me and my big foot." Sarah's dad sat down on the sofa with his cup of tea. "I was only trying to be helpful."

"It's okay, Roy. I've already got a good idea. I'm going to be a bike courier."

"Ah well, now you're talking. If you need any help finding your way around, you only have to ask. No-one gets to drive a black cab in London without doing the Knowledge. I can soon teach you all you need to know."

Think about it ...

What do you think of Raj's job plans?

How easy do you think it is to combine school, a job, family and friends?

---

2 **cross** annoyed, angry – 7 **fees** the money paid to go to a university or private school –
12 **my big foot** from to put one's foot in one's mouth = to say the wrong thing
18 **the Knowledge** special test cab drivers in London have to pass

7 A new job

"Standa-ard! Evening Standa-ard. Read all about it! Mobile phone scam. Thousands of mobile phones stolen every week. Read all about it!"

Raj got out of the tube at Bond Street and walked down Oxford Street, past sandwich bars and cheap tourist shops selling London T-shirts and red London buses; past the large department stores, Selfridges, John Lewis, Debenhams.

It was late on Friday afternoon and the streets were full of shoppers. He crossed over the road at Oxford Circus and past Langham Place and the large stone buildings of the BBC. Maybe one day he would get work there, doing radio plays.

In his hand he had a computer print-out of SmartBike.co.uk. After a long search on the internet in the college library and lots of phone calls that morning, he now had an interview at the bike couriers SmartBike.co. He had missed his last lesson at college but he had decided it was worth it.

---

16 **scam** an illegal trick or action in order to make money – 27 **college** type of school where pupils go at 16 – 30 **to be worth it** when it is a good idea to spend time or money doing sth

He looked at his watch. It was 4.50 and he was supposed to be there at 5 o'clock. He mustn't be late. He looked through the pages of the A-Z. Wardour Street. 37b Wardour Street.

Number 37 was a narrow building between a coffee shop and a Greek restaurant. Raj pressed the buzzer.

"Come straight up. Second floor – red door."

The office was tiny. Two people were sitting at desks piled high with papers and computers. On the floor, there were black and red courier bags with SmartBike.co written on them. The phone was ringing all the time. Suddenly a young girl rushed in with one of the courier bags on her back.

"Ginger, take this to Union Street. Number 15. Books and Co." A man with a strong American accent gave the girl a pile of papers.

"Union Street. Oh that's by The Cut isn't it? Near the Young Vic Theatre."

Ginger stuffed the papers in her bag and ran out down the stairs. "See you later."

Raj was beginning to feel very small. He knew the Young Vic. He had been to that theatre a lot. But he didn't know all the names of the streets. How could he be a bike courier like that?

"So, you must be Raj. Hi, I'm Brad. You ever been a courier before? Do you know London well?"

He didn't wait for Raj to reply.

"The way it works: we pay you per job. The quicker you are, the more jobs you do and the more money you earn. Okay?"

Raj nodded. He decided it was best to say nothing.

"Now all our couriers cover a three square mile area. We are looking for someone to work along the South Bank from Waterloo Station down to Deptford and Greenwich. Where do you live Raj?"

---

3 **A-Z** book of street maps (here: of London) – 5 **buzzer** door bell – 7 **tiny** very small

"Willesden Green. NW10."

"Oh a North Londoner then. Do you know South London at all?"

"A bit. But I can learn."

"Fine. Now you said on the phone you can only work weekends. What about if you turn up here in the office at eight in the morning next Saturday? In a week. That'll be the 15th? We can give you the radio and bags and you can study your A-Z." He pointed at the book in Raj's top pocket. "You might be needing that."

Raj smiled. "Is that it? I mean, have I got the job?"

"Yup, it's yours. Just fill in this form before you go and we'll see you Saturday week."

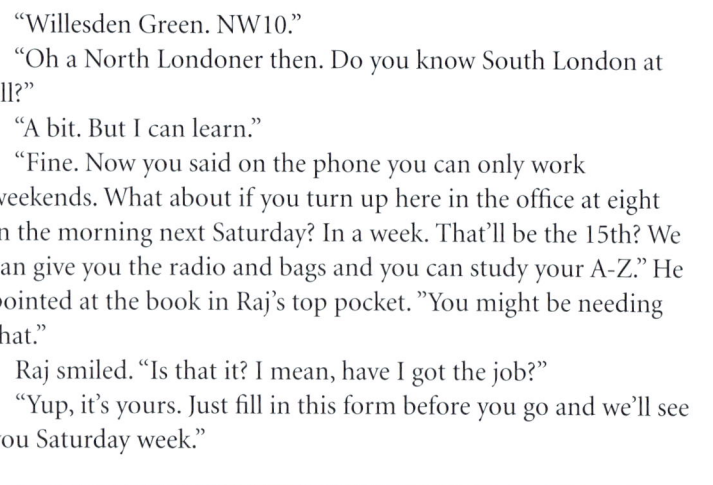

Think about it...

Raj needs to learn a lot - and very quickly. What advice would you give him?

8 The big day

Raj was up early the next morning. His father had already gone to work. Usually he would have gone with him. Meesha stuck her head out of the bedroom door as Raj went downstairs.

"So, it's the big day, isn't it? They're still mad at you, you know."

"Really?" He knew Meesha was enjoying the drama.

"Are you still going then?" she asked.

"Sure."

"So I've got to work in the shop later. Thanks, Raj."

"Look, I'll do it for you tomorrow ..."

"Forget tomorrow. Raj comes first, our Golden Boy! And is our First-born coming to the temple tonight?"

She slammed the bedroom door behind her.

Raj set off through the streets of Willesden towards the tube. He was Romeo in Verona going to meet his Juliet. Had he done enough to prepare? Was he good enough to get a place at drama school anyway? Would he get through to Round Three?

It was four stops on the Jubilee Line to Swiss Cottage. The tube was empty so Raj started practising his Shakespeare. A woman who got on at Kilburn quickly moved compartment at West Hampstead.

Raj walked through the Saturday market at Swiss Cottage. It was the usual mixture of wooden furniture, old cups and plates, fruit and vegetables and hot dogs. The smell of sausages made Raj feel sick.

As he walked up Eton Avenue he saw Michael sitting on the steps of the Central School of Speech and Drama. Michael was texting someone on his mobile.

"Hi," Raj said.

"Oh, hi." Michael didn't look up.

"Looks like we're the first," Raj said nervously. "Wonder if we are the only ones."

"Very unlikely. There are three thousand applicants each year and only twenty-five places."

Raj was beginning to feel very small. Raj opened his copy of Romeo and Juliet and went through his lines.

Raj looked up. There was a group of people coming up the road. Five men and two girls. They were chatting and laughing together. They looked like they knew each other already.

"Oh hi, I'm Patsy. Who are you?" said a pretty blonde woman with glasses.

"I'm Michael." He jumped up and shook her hand. "Are you here for the audition?" Suddenly Michael was very happy to speak.

"I'm Raj." But nobody took much notice.

Raj looked at the group that had just arrived. One of the men looked old enough to be his dad. There were two women, Patsy and a smaller woman called Georgia.

"What's the best part you've ever done?" asked Patsy.

A boy with dreadlocks ran up the steps and shouted "To be or not to be." Then he sat down again. "I played Hamlet at University."

---

7 **to text** to send sb a message with a mobile phone – 12 **applicant** person trying to get a job or a place at a school – 29 **dreadlocks** long hair which is twisted tightly into plaits or sections which hang down

"Oh that's funny," said Georgia. "I played Ophelia at the Edinburgh Festival this summer."

University? Edinburgh Festival? What were all these people doing here? They didn't need to go to drama school. They all had so much experience.

Suddenly the door opened and a man came out.

"Cor! He looks great." Patsy whispered to Georgia.

"Hi I'm Ned. Are you all here now? There should be nine of you. Yup, you can all come in then."

"Are you one of the teachers?" asked Georgia.

"No," Ned laughed. "I'm a third-year student here. I'm just here to tell you what you have to do today and to show you around. Come in and you can get a tea or coffee."

"How many places are there today?' the older man asked.

"I don't know. Sometimes they take three people – sometimes nobody is asked to stay. They know what they are looking for. It just depends if you've got it."

"Oh, that simple is it?"

"Right," Ned went on. "In a minute you will all go into the main theatre. You will do your Shakespeare piece on the stage in front of the three tutors and in front of everybody else. Then they will ask you to do some improvisation. I'll tell you who is going first in a second. Where's my list?"

"Is this it?" Michael asked.

"Oh yes. Er, who's Raj? You're number one."

Suddenly the two wooden doors opened and one of the teachers came out.

"We're ready for you now. Would you all like to come in and Raj would you take a place on the stage? I am the director of the theatre school. My name is Simon Barnes. With me are Pamela Stephenson – our voice coach – and Richard Grey, our dance tutor."

2 **Edinburgh Festival** very important Scottish music and theatre festival – 7 **cor** sl expression of surprise: wow – 31 **voice coach** sb who teaches actors how to speak properly

Raj was starting to feel sick. His legs felt like jelly and he was finding it difficult to breathe. He walked down the long red carpet steps towards the front. There were three teachers at a table near the back of the theatre. The other students were all sitting around the auditorium. Raj climbed up the steps onto the stage. As he took his place in the middle, he suddenly knew why he was there. He remembered his dad and the shop. He thought about selling lottery tickets and Sunday papers for the rest of his life. "I'm going to be an actor and nothing is going to stop me," he thought. He took a long deep breath, sat down on the floor at the front of the stage and began to speak.

Think about it ...

What would you do to prepare for an audition?

---

1 **like jelly** here: very weak

9 Another Romeo

"So last but not least, that's number nine – Michael Hills. Can you please come and do your monologue?" Suddenly Michael didn't look so confident. He smiled at the teachers and started speaking. He was doing a piece from Romeo and Juliet as well. Another Romeo. After a few seconds one of the teachers stood up.

"Michael. This is a large theatre. We can't hear you at the back. Start again. Take your time. And please speak up."

Raj looked closely at Michael. He was so glad that this hadn't happened to him. Surely it meant Michael wouldn't get a place now? Secretly, Raj felt glad.

"Heaven is here,
Where Juliet lives, and every cat and dog
And little mouse, every unworthy thing,
Live here in heaven and may look on her."

By now Michael was on the ground and was crying. Everyone in the room was watching him very carefully. Raj knew that Michael really could act.

"So, all of you, well done. Could you all please go and sit on the stage and then I will explain what we would like you to do next. Raj, I would like you to begin again. I want you to take another speech of Romeo's. Here it is." He handed Raj a piece of paper. "Imagine you are Romeo. A modern Romeo. You have just met the most lovely girl and you are telling your best friend about her. You are sitting on a park bench."

For some reason Raj suddenly thought of Sarah. He imagined he was telling a friend about her. He sat with his feet on a chair and started speaking. He was reading the speech Michael had just done. Raj knew everyone was looking at him. And it felt good. He knew his Romeo was just as good as Michael's.

The next hour passed in a blur for Raj. He watched the other eight actors do their Shakespeare pieces in a bath, at a circus or on the top of a bus. They all seemed very good. Raj knew it was going to be difficult to get another recall.

3 **confident** very certain of oneself

"Okay guys," the director suddenly jumped up and stood on his chair. "We would like to take an hour's break so we can talk about all the pieces." He suddenly pointed to Ned. "Could you please show them all where they can go and get a sandwich? Then can we see you all back here at 2 o'clock."

Raj couldn't believe it. Another sixty minutes to wait. Another sixty minutes to worry.

"I would just like to say thank you for your time today. We have seen some very interesting work." Simon Barnes was sitting on the front of the stage and talking in a very quiet but serious voice.

"It's been a difficult decision but one that we have all agreed on. We would like to see Raj and Michael again for another recall on Friday 29th October – a nice early start – at 8 in the morning. The rest of you. Thank you very much. And good luck with your other auditions."

Everyone left the auditorium in silence. Ned was at the door smiling at Raj and Michael.

"Well done. Good work."

"Cheers," Michael said.

"Thanks. I can't believe it," said Raj.

"What's the matter, Raj. You don't look very pleased. Just think, the next audition could be the last one. If you get through that, you could get a place here."

"Yes, but how am I going to pay for it?"

Raj walked in a daze to the tube station. For a moment he was enjoying the dream.

Think about it ...

Raj's dream is one step closer to reality. Think of three adjectives that best describe the way Raj is feeling.

19 **cheers** (informal) thanks – 21 **pleased** happy – 25 **in a daze** feeling confused

10 The Temple

Raj had been too excited to go straight home and had instead
taken the 260 bus towards Golders Hill.

From there he had walked miles through Golders Hill Park
and into Hampstead Heath until he had finally found a bench
at the top of Parliament Hill. He watched happy families flying
kites and the dogs chasing each other. In the distance he could see
Canary Wharf and the Pyramid tower, to the right of them Big
Ben and even nearer the Old Post Office Tower.

He took out the A-Z and studied the roads. New Globe Walk,
Bear Gardens, Clink Street, Tower Bridge Road, Tooley Street.
Soon Raj would know all these streets like the back of his hand.

It was after six o'clock when he got home and the house
was very quiet. Raj was surprised no-one was in. His parents
never worked Saturday evening. There was no dal on the stove,

---

22 **to fly kites** material on string which flies when the wind is strong – 28 **to know sth
like the back of your hand** to be very familiar with sth

no chapattis on the table – and no lassi in the fridge. Then he remembered: Neasden Temple.

Raj got his bike from the garage and cycled like a madman through the streets of Willesden and Neasden. There was a special ceremony tonight. All his uncles, aunts and cousins would be there. He couldn't miss it.

Special lanterns were hanging in front of the Shree Swaminarayan Mandir, the largest Hindu temple outside India. The lights were shining brightly and the sound of the music rang out. Raj took off his shoes and climbed the stairs to the prayer hall. The ceremony had already started. He saw his mother and sister and his two aunts kneeling on one side of the room. He joined his father and uncles who were on the ground praying. He didn't look at his father but stared ahead at the statues of the gods: Ganesh, Shiva and Vishnu. The smell of incense filled the air. Raj was so tired that he began to feel quite dizzy with the smell. Large baskets of food were handed out. Raj ate the samosas and bhajis in two bites and began to feel better. He saw his mother and sis-ter staring at him. Then his mother came over.

"Thank you," she said and gave him a big hug. It felt good to be held by her. "Thank you for coming."

Think about it ...

How do you think Raj's family will react if he isn't there?

What kind of family gatherings do you have?
How important are they for your family?

---

1 **chapatti** round flat Indian bread – 1 **lassi** Indian yoghurt drink – 12 **to kneel** to go down on your knees – 15 **incense** a substance that is burnt to produce a sweet smell – 16 **dizzy** feeling as if everything is spinning around – 17 **samosa** Indian snack, filled with spicy vegetables or meat – 20 **to hug** to put your arms around sb warmly

11 Waterloo Station

"We'll start at Waterloo Station. No better place to begin on the South Bank really." Sarah's dad shouted over his shoulder. He was driving over the bridge with Raj sitting behind him in the black cab. He could see St Paul's to the left and straight ahead the red digital sign on the front of the National Theatre. And to the right, the London Eye was still moving very slowly.

"I've got an hour before I start work. So you'll have to learn quickly, Raj."

Raj nodded.

"You know Waterloo Station, and the international terminal. You don't need to take the main entrance. There are lots of great short cuts you can use. See that flight of steps, carry your bike down there and you're right on the South Bank. Thirty minutes and you'll be in Greenwich."

Raj was making notes in his book.

"And if you're feeling tired – or you want a quick getaway – I guess you can always take one of the river boats."

25 **terminal** place where trains or planes leave or arrive – 28 **South Bank** cultural centre of South London on the banks of the River Thames

The cab turned sharply at the end of Waterloo Bridge. "You know what that is, don't you. You'll be dropping off messages for the stars here."

"Why, what's that?"

"Thames TV, next to the OXO Tower."

"What about the Millennium Bridge? Can I cycle over that?" Raj asked.

"No it's just for pedestrians. But I guess you could always push your bike along it. That takes you to St Paul's Cathedral and into the City of London."

"What about the route to Greenwich?" Raj asked.

"Oh yes, it takes you around the back of Southwark. Follow those signs there to the Globe."

"Do I go down Tooley Street and Jamaica Street?" Raj asked, looking at the same time at the map.

"You shouldn't need to. Look , we're in Bermondsey now – just across the river from Wapping – news-paper land. You can pick up your bargains here. Cheaper than Portobello anyway. You can take the roads right by the river – Bermondsey Wall East and through Southwark Park. But don't end up down the Rotherhithe Tunnel. That's not much fun on the bike."

"This is great, Roy. I'm beginning to learn the names."

"Oh you will in time. You might learn a lot more, too. There's a lot of history around here. There's all the old warehouses – and Clink Prison, of course. Don't get stuck in there. Cor, look at the time. I'd better drop you off. We'll go back the quick way via Elephant and Castle. Must be one of the worst examples of modern architecture. A big pink shopping centre. Look, there it is. Don't cycle down here – it's a death trap. Anyway, you're on

---

8 **pedestrians** people going on foot – 13 **the Globe** reconstruction of Shakespeare's theatre on the banks of the River Thames – 18 **bargain** sth you can buy at a very cheap price – 18 **Portobello (Road)** famous street market in North London – 29 **it's a death trap** it's very dangerous

your own now, Raj. I'll leave you at London Bridge. You can get the Jubilee Line home from here."

"Thanks a lot, Roy. I'll let you know how I get on."

"I'm sure you will, Raj."

"And if you speak to my daughter, can you tell her to do some work? I don't know when any of you get any college work done. See you later."

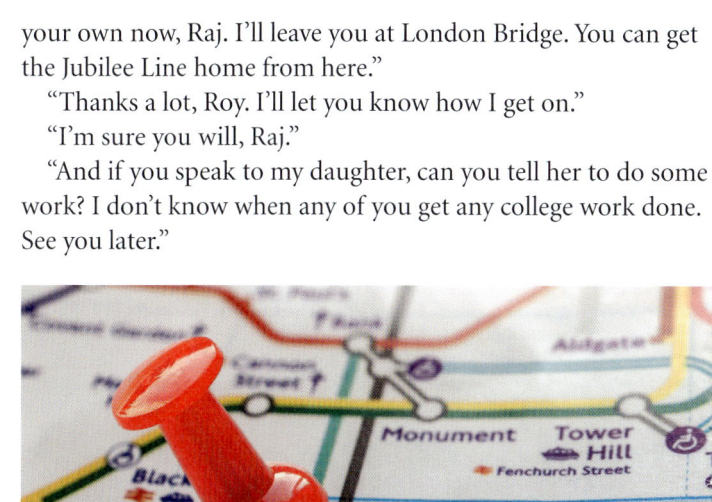

Think about it...

> When do think Sarah and Raj have time to do their school work?

> When do you have time for your homework and revision?

12 Day one

"That's the form. Just fill in all the details you can. We'll need your national insurance number. And if you haven't got any bike insurance – you can fill in this form, too."

Brad, the American, was sitting on the desk, the phone in one hand and a large cup of cappucino in the other.

"Yes, sorry. Hello, Smart Bike." Brad made a sign to Raj to hurry up with the form. He then pointed to the bike bags and the two-way radio.

"Norman Road. Number 23. Right. Yup. We've got the parcel. The courier's just left." The phone was ringing again. Brad pointed to Raj and told him to pick it up.

"Thirty minutes? Yeah, no problem."

"Hello, Smart Bike. Eh – just a minute." Raj handed the phone to Brad.

"Right," Brad said and held his hand over the phone. "You done the form? Good. Got the address – Norman Road. Number 23."

Raj put the bag over his shoulder and went towards the door.

"Hey, Raj, hold it – another job for you."

Raj stood still. Two jobs already and it was only five past eight.

"Okay new customer. Very important you get this one right. It's in Convoy's Wharf, Deptford. Unit 33. Got to impress a new customer. Then they'll keep coming back."

Raj wrote it down.

"What am I taking?"

"Nothing. They'll have something for you. Let me know on the radio when you're finished there. I'll probably have the next job for you. Oh, and one more thing."

"Yes?"

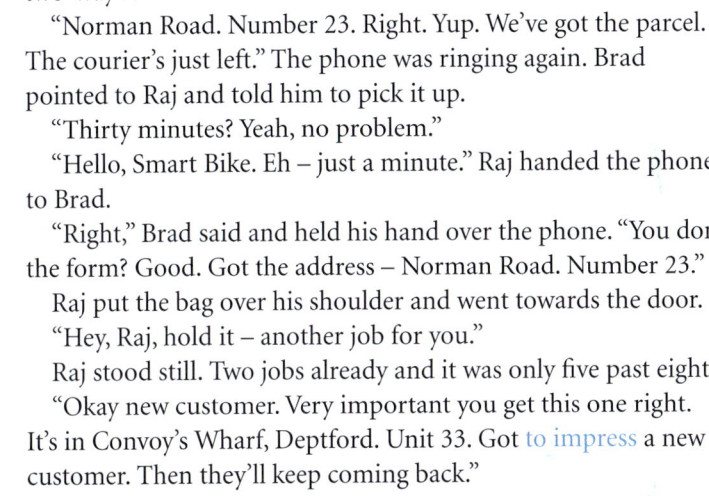

---

2 **national insurance number** identification number from the government you need when you start a job – 3 **insurance** money paid in case sth is lost or stolen or in case sb gets hurt – 21 **to impress** to make sb think good things about sth

"Make sure they sign these forms when you leave the parcel. Name, signature and date and time. Very important. Well, go on then – what are you waiting for? Time is money."

Think about it...

Do you think Raj know enough about the job to be able to do it well?

13 The first fiver

The Strand, the Aldwych, Waterloo Bridge. "Down the steps and onto the South Bank." Roy's words were still ringing in his ears. The man selling second-hand books was putting up his stall outside the National Film Theatre. There were one or two people walking home from the night before – and a few drunks. Otherwise the South Bank was empty. The theatres and museums were shut. The skateboar-ders and musicians were still in bed.

In twenty minutes Raj was in Deptford and on the way to Norman Road. Taking out the yellow packet from his bag, he tied his bike up.

"Got a parcel for you. It's SmartBike." Raj shouted over the intercom.

"Fine. Come up."

"Please sign and write your name next to the date and time. ... Right, thanks a lot."

---

20 **drunk** sb who has drunk too much alcohol – 27 **intercom** sth that people speak into to communicate with sb who is inside/outside a building or in a different room

He ran down the steps two at a time. His first job. Raj had earned his first five pounds and it was only 8.30. He was beginning to enjoy this.

Convoy's Wharf was just round the corner. Raj was there in five minutes.

It was very different from the smart streets of Bermondsey. The streets were cobbled. There were burned-out cars, old bikes and an old bed on the ground. There was broken glass everywhere and street signs. It took Raj about ten minutes to find the place. He didn't have a name, just a number – Unit 33. There was no door, just a large steel gate. Raj looked around for a bell or a buzzer. Finally, he saw one around the corner.

"Hello, it's SmartBike. I've come to get a parcel from you." Raj could hear the chain rattling as the steel door started opening.

"It's the second door on the right," a voice said. "Turn left at the end of the corridor and then take the red door."

It was an odd place. Raj had no idea what they sold or made here. But he remembered what Brad said. It's very important to get the first job right.

A small fat man was sitting at a desk and smoking a cigar. There were piles of mobile phones on the desk.

He took a long hard look at Raj and told him to sit down. Raj looked around him. Apart from the desk and the chair the man was sitting on, there was no other furniture in the room. The man told him to wait a second and he disappeared. He came back with another chair and a cup of coffee for Raj.

"Coffee?"

"Thanks." Raj didn't think he could say no. But he wanted to go. He needed to be on his bike and making more money.

"I'm Ed. I'm the boss here. What's your name?"

"Raj."

"Have you been doing this a long time?"

"No, it's my first day."

The man smiled.

"I see. So you want to do well?"

There was something strange about Ed, but he didn't know what.

"This is a new business. We are looking for a bike courier we can trust. For the right person, there's lots of money to be made."

Raj liked the sound of it.

"Need a new mobile, Raj? Have this one. It's the latest model."

"I haven't got the money. I really don't need a new phone."

"Take it. It's a present. I like you, Raj. And when Ed likes someone, he wants to help them. Let me just take the number down. If I've got an extra job for you – I can ring you directly or send you a text message. No need to bother SmartBike. You can earn more money that way."

Raj hesitated.

"Don't you want to earn lots of money, Raj?"

Raj thought of the place at drama school. Perhaps there wasn't a problem. He could work for Ed and SmartBike. And he could always say no. Ed didn't even know his surname or where he lived. All he had was the mobile number.

Suddenly there was a call on the two-way radio. Raj answered it.

"Yes, hello. Yes, I've finished there. It went fine. Bermondsey. Okay. Drummond Road. Number 7. Fine."

"Okay, Raj. I can see you're a busy man. See you again soon I hope."

"What about the parcel?"

"Oh yes, I nearly forgot. Can you take this to Druid Street? Number 22a. Ask for Mike."

18 **to hesitate** to be uncertain and therefore wait to do sth

Raj put the thin brown envelope in his bag with the mobile phone.

"Eh, can you sign this please and print your name?"

He felt stupid asking Ed to do this.

"You're quick to learn, aren't you. There you go."

Raj put the clipboard back in the bag. He tried to read the name on the form. It just said Ed.

He walked out of Unit 33 and got on his bike. He was glad to be on the road again. But he was also excited. Things were beginning to happen in his life.

Think about it ...

Do you like the sound of Raj's job?

---

6 **clipboard** small board that holds pieces of paper in position so you can write on them

14 Another friend?

"Where have you been? Why haven't you rung me? You don't want to know me now you've got your new job and your new theatre friends."

Sarah and Raj were sitting outside the College of North West London.

They had just had two hours of business studies.

"That's not true. And I don't have any new theatre friends. I haven't even got a place there yet."

"Well, what have you been doing? You never ring me anymore. Even Dad says he hasn't seen you for days."

"I've just been working. I need to make lots of money to pay for drama school. That's all."

Suddenly Raj's mobile phone rang. He looked at the screen. He knew that number. It was Ed's.

"Tonight. Eh. I don't know. What time? Yes okay."

Sarah went quiet. Then she asked.

"So, who are you seeing tonight?"

"No-one. I mean I'm just working."

"You've got a new phone. When did you buy that?"

"I didn't. It was a present."

Sarah stood up quickly.

"I've got to go. I've got some work to do. Ring me when you have some time."

Raj felt bad. He always told Sarah everything. Or most things. But he didn't think he could tell her about Ed. At least not yet.

Think about it ...

? How do you think Sarah is feeling?

15 An extra job

It was seven o'clock and Raj was sitting with his family having supper.

"Another good day. We've sold even more lottery tickets this week. Not changing your mind, Raj?"

It was a month since the big argument and Raj's father was beginning to talk to him. He never asked about the drama school. And he didn't even know about the cycle courier job. Raj had decided it was better to say nothing.

"Leave it, Ravi. We said we wouldn't talk about it any more."

"Not talk about my own business in my own house. The business that has been in the family for years."

Meesha turned to look at Raj for his reaction. His mother put her arm on Raj's shoulder.

"There's still a lot of time for that. Raj, more paratha?"

"No, thanks." Raj was looking at the clock. "I'm going out in a minute."

He had to be in Deptford at 8.30 and he needed to start moving now.

"Can't we have a family meal in this house? Where are you going? Don't you have any homework to do?"

"That's what I'm doing," said Raj. "I'm going to Sarah's house to discuss a project."

Raj hated telling lies. But he had no choice.

"Oooh, Sarah's again. Raj and Sarah. What a sweet pair." Meesha made a heart sign in the air.

"We're friends, Meesha, nothing more."

His mother winked at him.

"Raj hasn't got time for girls, Meesha. He has to concentrate on his studies," Raj's father added.

"That's right," said Raj. He grabbed his coat and his mobile phone.

"What about your school bag, Raj?" Meesha shouted.

---

27 **to wink** to shut one eye whilst keeping the other open

"Don't need it. The notes are at Sarah's house."

Raj walked to the tube. He had left his bike in the garage at the back of Wardour Street. On the way he rang Sarah's number. He didn't know what she would say.

"Sarah, it's Raj. I'm sorry about today. I need to ask you a favour."

"What now? I thought you had a hot date?"

"A date? No, you must be joking. It's a job. I can't speak now. I'll tell you tomorrow."

"When?"

"I don't know."

"One o'clock in Covent Garden. You can buy me lunch."

"Anything you say. Look, if you see my sister or my parents, we're spending the evening doing course work."

"Oh, Raj."

"Please."

"Okay. But I really do mean it about lunch."

"So do I. One o'clock outside Covent Garden tube station."

It was dark in Convoy's Wharf and at eight-thirty at night, the streets were empty. He rang the buzzer of Unit 33. No answer. He rang again. Still no answer. He was just about to go when he heard Ed's voice.

"Raj, come in. So pleased you could come."

Raj walked down the long empty corridors and into the office he had been in before. There was still no-one there. He could hear an argument in the room behind him. Suddenly Ed came in. He shook Raj's hand.

"Good man. First thing, does anyone know you are here. Parents? Brothers and sisters? Girlfriend?"

"No, no-one."

"Where did you leave your bike?"

"It's outside."

"Next time bring it in here, or leave it somewhere else."

"But won't I need it?"

"I'm not sure yet. I've got lots of jobs you can help me with."

Raj was feeling uneasy. What was going on?

"Raj, I've got to go out for a bit. Have you got your mobile phone?"

"Yes, it's here."

"Good. Good. I need you to answer the phone for me. I'm going to give you a password. It's 'Operation Spider'. When I ring in, I'll say, 'Operation Spider. The spider's left its web.' Ten minutes – and this is very important – ten minutes after this I want you to ring this number 07968 303 731 and say 'Operation Spider. The spider's got the fly.' Don't write the number down anywhere and don't tell anyone else this number. Have you got this?"

Raj nodded. But he didn't like the sound of this.

"But I'm a bike courier. Why ..."

Ed's smile disappeared.

"Don't worry, you can deliver a parcel for me at the end of the evening. Make yourself at home – there's some magazines on the floor over there. You can read them."

"But how long is this going to take? I've got to get the last tube home."

Ed was looking very cross now.

"Raj, we're friends. Let's stay friends. Your uncle Ed will pay for a black cab home if there's a problem. Don't worry."

And he walked out of the room and banged the door.

Raj heard some electric gates opening at the back of the building and a dog barking. Then what sounded like a large truck and a motorbike left at the same time. Then there was silence.

Raj was beginning to feel very uneasy. It was already 10.30 and he had had no phone call. At first he had walked back down the corridor to the entrance but it was locked. He couldn't get out. He was too scared to go anywhere else. As soon as he had moved he had heard the dog barking again.

---

1 **uneasy** uncomfortable or uncertain – 29 **entrance** way in

Raj looked through the magazines – sports magazines and film guides – but he couldn't concentrate.

He was just beginning to fall asleep on the desk, when his mobile phone started ringing. Raj started shaking. He answered the phone.

"Hello."

"Operation Spider. The spider's left its web."

The line went dead.

Raj looked at his watch. 10.43. It was a long ten minutes. At 10.53 he dialled the number. He had been saying it in his head all night so he wouldn't forget it. 07968 303 731.

Someone picked up the phone very quickly. He was surprised to hear a woman's voice saying "Yes?"

"Operation Spider," Raj said quietly. "The spider's got the fly." The phone went dead again.

It was ten to twelve before Raj saw Ed again. Raj heard the electric gates, the dog barking and the sound of the truck. Then Ed walked in. He threw a bag of crisps at Raj.

"Thought you might be hungry."

But Raj felt sick not hungry.

Ed took out a big black wallet. He counted out five twenty-pound notes and gave them to Raj. "That's for tonight. And here's another twenty-five pounds for the black cab. That should get you home. I'll see you to the door."

Raj jumped up. He couldn't get out of there quickly enough.

Ed held Raj's hand at the door.

"Good work, Raj. Very good work. You'll hear from me again."

Raj ran down the street to his bike. He was shaking so much he couldn't undo the lock. It was only as he was cycling to Waterloo that he realized he hadn't even taken a parcel for Ed. So why did Ed need a bike courier?

It was so late that Raj realized he would miss the last tube. Instead he went to the taxi rank at Waterloo Station. He knew he could put his bike in the back of a black cab. As he stood waiting there, he wondered what he would say if Sarah's Dad picked him up. But it was a woman driving the cab.

"Where are you going?"

"Willesden Green. NW10."

"Hmm. Don't normally go that far. It's expensive you know. Can you afford it? It'll be more than twenty pounds with the bike."

"That's okay. I've got the money."

Raj held up two twenty pound notes.

"Okay, Willesden it is."

? Think about it ...

At what stage do you think that Raj realises that the work he's doing is not legal?

What would you do in his shoes?

2 **wallet** sth you can keep money in – 10 **to undo** to open

16 Lunch

"I still don't understand why we've got to eat lunch outside," Sarah moaned. "It's freezing. Are you mad?"

"I know. But I can't talk in there."

Raj and Sarah were the only people sitting at tables opposite the Theatre Museum.

"So," Sarah said, "what's the story?"

Raj sighed. He still didn't know what to say. Ed had said he mustn't tell anyone, but Raj's head was bursting.

"Look, Sarah, I think I'm in trouble."

Sarah gasped. "Why? What have you done?"

Raj took a deep breath, then he began to talk. He didn't stop for ten minutes.

"What am I going to do?"

Sarah put her head in her hands. "Oh Raj, that's awful. You must go to the police."

"No," Raj shouted. Then he said more quietly. "No, I can't. I don't really know what they're doing there. Maybe there's nothing wrong. And anyway the police won't believe me – a young Asian boy."

"We could tell my dad?" Sarah said helpfully.

"No, you musn't."

"But what are you going to do? Operation Spider – nobody talks like that. Hey wait. I know, we could ring the number."

"But Ed told me to forget the number."

"He won't know it's you. We can use the phone box over there. They won't be able to trace the number then. Come on." Sarah was already running to the phone.

"Look, I don't think this is a good idea ..."

"The number?"

"07968 303 731."

Sarah dialled it. Then she put the phone down.

"No answer. The line's dead."

---

2 **to moan** to complain about sth – 10 **to gasp** to open your mouth in surprise or shock –
26 **to trace** here: to find out

17 The next call

Three weeks later and there had been no more phone calls. Raj had worked at SmartBike every Saturday and Sunday. Brad was very pleased with him and he was beginning to make quite a lot of money. Maybe he could afford to go to drama school after all.

Then on Thursday, 28th October, just as he was walking to college, Raj's phone rang. He had almost stopped carrying it with him as he had heard nothing from Ed. It was the day before his last audition at the Central School of Speech and Drama. It was also Divali. Raj knew who was ringing. No-one else had his number. He waited for ten rings. He hoped it would stop, but it didn't. Finally he answered it.

"Raj, it's Ed. You okay?"

"Yes." Raj knew he sounded nervous.

"Raj, I've got another job for you."

"When?"

"Tonight. It's very important."

Raj felt sick. Tomorrow was the most important day in his life – a last audition at drama school. He needed to go to bed early tonight and practise his pieces. He didn't want to spend the night in a warehouse. Raj tried to sound friendly but firm.

"I'm really sorry, Ed. Tonight's no good for me. Sorry about that."

"Raj, I'm sorry. You are working tonight. Nothing can be more important. Do you want me to ring Smart Bike and tell them what you've been doing?"

Raj said nothing.

"No, I thought not. Can I trust you, Raj? Nine o'clock at Unit 33. And don't worry – it won't be a late night."

The phone went dead. Raj felt dizzy. The most important day of his life – and he would be exhausted.

30 **exhausted** very tired

Raj couldn't concentrate at college. He could hear Neil Young's words" VAT. How important is it for the economy? Raj? Raj, are you listening? Are you with us today?"

Suddenly Raj realized everyone was looking at him. Again he had no idea what to say.

"Raj come and see me at the end of the lesson. I think we need to have a serious talk."

That was the last thing Raj needed. All he wanted to do was to have a serious talk with Sarah. He decided someone needed to know where he was going tonight – and he couldn't begin to tell his parents.

Just before the end of the lesson, he passed Sarah a note. IMPORTANT. BIG TROUBLE. MEET ME AT THE SIDE STEPS. Sarah nodded and sent him back a note. I'LL WAIT TILL YOU COME OUT.

At the end of Business Studies, Raj went to see Neil Young. But he didn't have much to say.

"Raj, we've got exams in two weeks. If you want to pass the exam, it would be a good idea if you started to do some work." And he left the room.

"Oh, Sarah. What can I do?" Sarah handed Raj a hot coffee.

"Has he rung again?" Raj nodded. They were sitting on some stone steps at the side of the building. It was getting cold now so there was no-one else outside. Sarah was holding her knees, trying to keep warm. Raj warmed his hands on his coffee. He explained what had happened.

"Oh Raj, you can't go. What if they do something awful to you?"

"But what if they do something awful to me anyway?"

"But they don't know where you live."

"No, but they could ring SmartBike. I bet Ed could easily find my address. And what if my parents found out? No, I'm going

2 **VAT** value added tax, a tax paid on all goods and services – 10 **he couldn't begin** he would find it impossible to

to go, but I'll give you my mobile phone number. If you haven't
heard from me by midnight tonight, then you can call your dad."

"What's the address of the place?"

"Unit 33, Convoy's Wharf in Deptford."

Raj cycled over Waterloo Bridge, past the red signs of the
National Theatre and along the South Bank. There were crowds
of people by the banks of the river outside the Royal Festival Hall.
It must be the interval, Raj thought. How he wished he was just
spending the evening watching a play or listening to some music.

He tried to practise his Shakespeare for the morning, but the
same bits of Romeo kept filling his head.

"Let me be taken, let me be put to death,
I am content, so thou will have it so."

He could hear the sound of fireworks in the distance. There
were rockets going off every few seconds for Divali. Then the

24 **interval** break in a play or concert

night sky was filled with bright lights. His parents would be celebrating at the Temple tonight.

Raj passed Gabriel's Wharf. Again there were crowds of people queuing up outside a restaurant or enjoying a drink in the cold night air. Raj began to feel very much alone – just like Romeo.

"Come death and welcome, Juliet wills it so."

The streets got more and more empty the nearer he got to Deptford. A motorcyclist suddenly raced past him. Then it was quiet again. He heard a dog barking and the sound of a train. Raj hid his bike around the corner of Convoy's Wharf down the side of a building. He didn't lock it. Then he walked very slowly to Unit 33. He felt the mobile phone in his pocket. It felt reassuring. At least Sarah had his number.

"Hello, it's Raj." This time, the metal door opened immediately. Ed and a very large man dressed in black leather were waiting for him when he came in. Ed looked nervous. It was the first time Raj had seen him like that.

"So, this is the boy. Thought he was supposed to be older? Are you sure we can trust him?" The man in leather sounded annoyed. Ed nodded.

"No-one knows you're here, do they Raj?" Ed asked.

"No," Raj said quietly. He knew he had to lie. A large Rottweiler dog was standing behind him, growling.

"Put a sock in it, Horace," the man in leather said. The dog walked away and sat down in the corner.

"Look, Frank, I'll speak to the boy. You go and get the truck ready. Come on, Raj, come to my office. We've got a big order tonight. I'm going to need your help."

Tonight the office was full of large brown boxes. HANDLE WITH CARE and THIS WAY UP were written on the side. But it didn't say what was inside them. Raj knew he couldn't ask.

---

12 **reassuring** comforting – 23 **to growl** to make an angry noise – 24 **Put a sock in it.** Shut up.

"I've got a client coming tonight to pick up these boxes. I need your help. Frank and I are busy. We've got to go out this evening. I need you to answer the phones for me again, and to be here when the client comes. Can I trust you?"

Raj didn't say anything. He felt uneasy. Why was a client collecting boxes after nine on a Thursday evening? And what was in these boxes anyway?

"Look, Ed, I don't think this is a good idea."

"Sorry, Raj, it's too late now. You're one of us. So don't go all soft on us and ring your mum, will you? And let's keep the police out of it, too, eh?"

Raj stared at the floor. This was awful. He was now a criminal, too. But how had this happened? And how was he going to get out of here?

Suddenly the red door opened and the man in leather, Frank, was back again.

"So, does he know what to do?"

"Just give me thirty seconds, Frank."

Frank left the room through the back door.

"Right," Ed said. He grabbed Raj's hand and held it very tight.

"You get it right tonight, and there's five hundred pounds for you. You mess up, and it's a life behind bars. Understand me now?"

Raj nodded. Ed put his arm around him. "Good lad. You've got two small things to do. When I ring you, I will give you the code word. 'Operation Spider. The spider's left the web.' I want you to ring a number for me fifteen minutes later. A different one this time: 07986 207705. Again I want you to say 'Operation Spider. The spider's got the fly.' Like last time, I want you to forget the number afterwards. Okay?"

22 **to mess up** to make a mistake – 22 **behind bars** in prison

Raj nodded again. He couldn't say anything as he was fighting back tears. But he didn't want Ed to see he was so upset.

"The client should be here soon afterwards. There will be two of them. When they ring the bell at the back, you let them in. You push the red button on the wall here. Whatever you do, don't press the blue button."

Ed grabbed a motorbike helmet from under a pile of boxes and went towards the door.

"Oh, and one last thing, Raj, don't try and run away. There's no way out." He smiled and then left the room. He turned the key in the lock behind him.

Raj heard the truck and the motorbike start up and the dog barking again. Then there was silence again. Raj didn't know what to do. There was nowhere to sit with all the boxes in the room, so he decided to explore. He walked back down the corridor the way he had always come in, but there were no secret doors. Raj walked back again into the room with the boxes. He tried the back door that Frank and Ed had used to get out to the truck. He knew that Ed had locked it when he left, but he tried it anyway.

He decided to send Sarah a message. He typed nervously. His fingers could hardly press the buttons.

Think about it …

If you were Raj, would you try to run away?

What would you do?

18 Worried sick

Sarah was sitting at her computer trying to do her Business Studies project, but she couldn't concentrate. There was the sound of fireworks everywhere. It seemed like everyone around her was celebrating the Festival of Lights tonight. All she could think of was Raj and Unit 33. Suddenly the phone rang. It was Raj's mother.

"No, sorry. I haven't seen Raj. ... No, he's not here. ... Oh, Divali, of course. ... Well, I'm sure he hasn't forgotten."

Sarah hated telling lies. But she couldn't tell Raj's mother that instead of celebrating Divali at Neasden Temple, he was in a warehouse somewhere in South East London.

She decided to give up on the Business Studies and went and ran a bath instead. Just as she was getting undressed, her phone went again. It was a text message. Sarah immediately knew who was sending it. It was what she was afraid of.

"Trbl. Tl ur dad. Cal l8r. Dnt rng me"

Sarah put her clothes back on and rang her dad. His phone was switched off. And she had no idea where in London he was working. All she could do was wait.

As soon as he had sent the message, Raj's phone rang. Raj felt sure someone was watching him. He waited for five rings, then he answered it.

"Hello."

The line went dead. "Hello. Hello." Raj was really nervous now.

Then a few minutes later the phone rang again. It was Ed.

"Bit of a hitch with Operation Spider. Ring the number. Tell them the spider will be on its way soon. I'll call you back."

Raj was really nervous now. What did all this mean?

He typed in the number. 07986 207 ... Then he couldn't remember. Was it 705 or 507? He tried 507 first, but the number didn't work. He dialled again – 07986 207705. It rang. A man answered the phone.

---

13 **to run a bath** to let water flow into a bathtub – 26 **bit of a hitch** there's a problem or difficulty

"The spider will be on its way soon," Raj said.

"What? What did you say? Has it left its web?" The man shouted. "Yes or no?"

"Eh, no, there's been a bit of a hitch," Raj said.

"What kind of hitch?"

"I don't know."

The line went dead again. Raj's head was spinning. What was he doing here? He decided he needed to know more. Raj sat down on the floor among the piles of boxes. One of the lids was loose. He lifted the lid carefully. His hands were sweating. He was sure his phone would ring again. But there was silence. Inside the box were rows and rows of mobile phones. All different shapes and sizes. Some of them looked just like the phone in his pocket. A slim silver one. He felt sick. He lay down on the floor among the boxes. What was he going to do now?

Somehow he must have fallen asleep. He suddenly woke when he heard the sound of a truck. It sounded different this time. He

---

7 **to spin** to go round and round – 32 **somehow** for some reason

looked at his watch, it was already 1.30. Raj must have been asleep for hours. Then he heard a bell ringing. He realized it was coming from the back of the warehouse. Raj pressed the red button. He heard the electric gate at the back opening and a truck driving in. Then the door at the back of the office was unlocked and two men walked in. Raj took a good look at them. One was very tall with long dark hair and a large tattoo on his arm with the word HORSE on it. The other man was smaller with bright blue eyes and a beard.

"This them?" The man with the beard asked and pointed to the boxes.

Raj nodded.

"Open up the warehouse, will you?"

Raj didn't know what they meant.

"Well, come on, are you stupid or something? The blue button."

Raj nodded and pressed the button. "You can give Horse and me a hand with these boxes, too. We've got to make the ferry in six hours. We'll never get to Dover otherwise."

Raj followed the two men out of the back of the room and into the warehouse at the back. He saw a large truck sitting there. An electric gate was opening to the right of the truck. Behind it there was another enormous room with yet more boxes in it. There must have been thousands of boxes in it.

"Come on, then," Horse said. "Follow me."

Raj looked at his watch. It was 5.30 and nearly morning. They hadbeen loading boxes for nearly four hours. All the boxes were now on the truck. The two men, Horse and Bob, were chatting and smoking a cigarette. Raj hadn't heard from Ed again. He didn't know what that meant. He felt exhausted. In two and a half hours I am supposed to be at the Central School of Speech

---

3 **warehouse** building where a shop keeps things it sells Warenlager – 18 **to make the ferry** to get the ferry in time

and Drama, he thought. And I'm stuck in a warehouse with some crooks in South London. Suddenly there was the sound of a police car. The small man with the beard came over to him. He handed him a big key ring and took him around the side of the truck.

"You can use that little silver key to open the door over there."

He pointed to a small grey door in the corner of the room. Raj hadn't noticed the door with the truck in the way.

"Just walk around the corner and see if the police have gone. They won't know you. Then come back and tell us. We need to go, if we want to make the ferry."

Raj nodded. He turned the key and disappeared around the corner. There was no sign of the police. He just had time to send Sarah a quick message.

"OK. Wtrlu Brg 15 mns. Stps"

He ran back into the warehouse.

"Is it safe?" the tall man asked. Raj nodded.

"Lock the door and give us the key again."

This was Raj's one big chance. He now knew there was only one way out. Raj pretended to lock the door, but left it open. Then he walked over to the two men.

"Here you are, your keys."

"You'll let us out won't you?"

"Sure."

Raj went back into the little office and pressed the red buzzer to let the truck out. It shut automatically once the truck had driven away.

Raj was just about to leave the office, when his phone went again. He looked at the screen. It was Ed's number. He didn't know whether to pick it up or not.

"Operation Spider. The Spider's left its web." Again the line went dead. He decided he would have to wait ten minutes before

2 **crook** criminal – 4 **key ring** sth you can put lots of keys on to keep them together

he rang the other number. He stood in the back of the warehouse next to the small grey door. After eight minutes he couldn't wait any longer and he took out his mobile phone again. It was now 6.05. He pressed the buttons 07986 207705. He had no problem remembering the number this time. He had written it on his arm.

"Operation Spider. The spider's got the fly." The line went dead again. Then Raj heard the sound of a motorbike. The electric gate began to open. Ed was back.

Think about it...

What do you understand about Operation Spider?

19 The race against time

Raj only had a few seconds to think. He knew the only way out was through the small grey door. He crouched down beside it. It was still quite dark in the warehouse. There was a chance that Ed wouldn't see him. Ed put his motorbike next to the wall and took off his helmet. Ed looked around him before he went into the office. He was obviously looking for Raj.

At that moment Raj pushed the grey door open and ran down the street. His heart was beating fast. He ran down the side of the building and jumped on his bike.

Raj knew that he now had to remember everything he had learned in the past few weeks working for SmartBike. There was no way he could be quicker than Ed's motorbike, but he could be smarter. Raj knew there were some routes he could take that a motorbike couldn't. But there was no doubt in his mind. He was in real danger. He headed for the river path. Suddenly he heard the sound of a motorbike starting. There was no doubt in his mind. Ed was after him.

The street lights were still on but the sun was slowly coming up. Raj tried to cycle in the shadows. It was only a twenty minute cycle to the steps at Waterloo Bridge and Roy's cab. But it was going to be a long twenty minutes.

Raj cycled along the back of Convoy's Wharf and through the playground at Pepys Park. He could hear the distant sound of a motorbike and he looked around him. Still no sign of Ed. As he came out of the park he went the wrong way. Suddenly he was on a larger road, Grove Street. Ed was just behind him. He could hear Ed shouting something, but he didn't know what he was saying. Raj didn't wait to find out.

Raj knew he had to get to the marina at South Dock and Greenland Dock. There were cycle paths all around the back of the sailing school.

---

13 **smarter** more intelligent – 29 **marina** place where boats can park

At the docks he lost Ed again. Ed must have decided to take the main road. There were lots of houses here and a man on a motorbike riding along the pavement at this time in the morning would have been an unusual sight. Ed wouldn't have wanted that. Raj weaved his way along the narrow paths by the side of the river, past Limehouse Beach towards Bermondsey. Still no sign of Ed. He could see London Bridge ahead of him. Only another ten minutes and I'm at Waterloo, he thought. Raj had never cycled so fast in his life. His lungs were burning with pain. Then suddenly Raj panicked. He could see Ed sitting on his motorbike on London Bridge. Next to him, on another motorbike, was Frank. They were waiting for him. Raj had no hope of beating two of them. The chase was over.

Raj was about to give up. He was exhausted. He didn't know where he could cycle to get away from them, when he suddenly saw the river boat at London Bridge. It was taking commuters to work in Blackfriars. If Raj could take his bike on the boat he

3 **pavement** path where people walk, next to the road – 4 **to weave** to move from side to side

could cycle from Blackfriars Bridge to Waterloo. There was a chance Ed and Frank still hadn't seen him.

Raj queued up to get his ticket.

"One to Blackfriars, please."

"You're not taking that bike are you? No way. Not between 6.30 and 9."

It was 6.40. The boat was leaving at 6.42. He could see it coming in from St Catherine's Dock.

"No, I'm leaving it over there," Raj said.

He dodged past the commuters and ran towards the pontoon. He knew he had to get on the boat. He pushed his way on.

"Hey you can't come on the boat with that bike."

"The man at the ticket office said I could today. I won't bring it again. Please. Look the boat's nearly empty."

Raj must have sounded desperate because the ticket collector let him on.

"Well, okay. But leave it over there on the luggage rack. If I ever see you again on here with a bike …"

As the boat started moving, Raj's phone started ringing. There was a text message.

"Rj. U r in the spdrs web. No escp"

Raj put the phone back in his pocket. He looked at the timetable on the wall. It was only seven minutes to Blackfriar's Bridge. He had seven minutes to think what to do.

"Can you add the coconut to the dhokla, please Meesha?"

Meesha and her mother were up early making some food. All around them were decorations and Divali cards. There were balloons and tinsel in every room.

"How much food are we making?" Meesha asked. "I can't believe we need this much for the party. There's enough to feed five hundred."

---

10 **to dodge past** to avoid hitting sth or sb by moving to another side quickly –
10 **pontoon** floating container that supports a bridge – 15 **desperate** in despair –
17 **luggage rack** place on boat or train where bags are put – 25 **dhokla** Indian vegetarian dish – 28 **tinsel** long pieces of thin shiny material used as a decoration

"Oh rubbish, Meesha."

Raj's father came down the stairs.

"I've just been into Raj's room and he didn't come home last night. He has no respect for the family any more. How could he not come to the Temple last night?"

"There must be something wrong. He knows how important Divali is. He wouldn't miss it."

"Raj only has one idea in his head now and that is acting."

But Raj's mother looked worried. Even Meesha was a little uneasy.

"I'll wait till 7.30 and then I'll ring Sarah's mobile. Maybe she can help."

Raj could already see Blackfriars Bridge quite clearly. In five minutes, the boat would be alongside the pontoon. He had to think quickly. Raj rang Sarah's mobile. She answered straight away.

"Where are you? We're on Waterloo Bridge but we can't wait here much longer. There's so much traffic."

"I'm on a river boat coming into Blackfriars Bridge. I'm in big trouble. They're following me."

Raj heard Sarah talking to her dad. Roy grabbed the phone.

"We'll meet you at Blackfriars Bridge. Do they know where you are now?"

"I don't know. They're on two motorbikes. The last time I saw them they were on London Bridge. They're going to kill me."

"Don't worry. We'll get the police."

At 6.49 the boat pulled into Blackfriars. The next few minutes passed in a dream. Raj pushed his bike up the pontoon along with the early morning commuters. Sarah and her dad were waiting for him. Raj was so relieved to see them. He ran towards them with his bike. Suddenly he heard a voice he recognized all too well.

"Hello, Raj. I think we need a word."

A leather glove dragged his arm to one side. His bike was thrown to the ground. He was face to face with Ed.

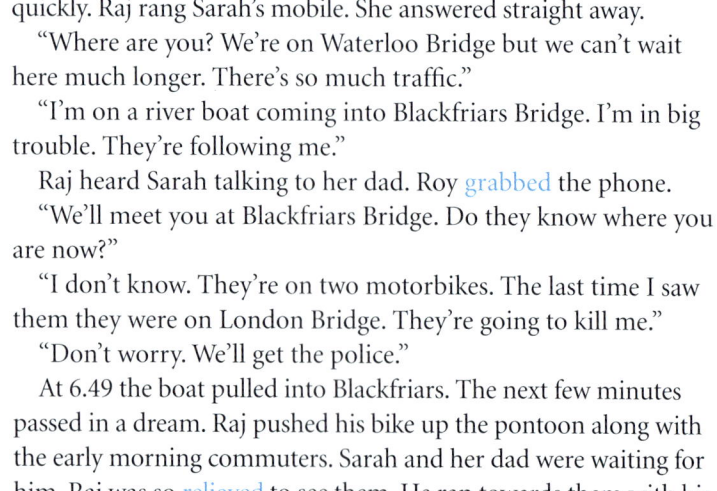

---

19 **to grab** to take sth quickly – 28 **relieved** no longer worried – 31 **to drag** to pull

"Hey wait a minute you two. Leave him alone." Roy tried to push them to one side.

"Who are you?" Ed asked. But there was no time to answer, Frank had punched Roy in the face. Sarah screamed. Raj thought he was about to faint. Then three police cars screeched to a halt. Six police officers ran onto the pontoon and pushed Ed and Frank to the floor.

"The game's over, boys."

Think about it ...

Why do you think Meesha wants to wait before calling Sarah?

---

5 **to faint** to feel dizzy and fall down; to lose consciousness – 5 **to screech to a halt** to stop suddenly so that the car makes a loud noise

20 Central School again

Raj, Sarah and her dad were drinking tea and eating biscuits at Blackfriars Police Station. Raj had spent the last thirty minutes telling them all about Unit 33. He had described the two men, Operation Spider and the truck full of boxes.

"We'll phone the police in Calais. They'll arrest the other two men when they get to France. Good work, Raj. If this is what we think it is, there could be a big reward for you. Half the Metropolitan Police have been after this gang for over a year. We believe these men have been stealing thousands of mobile phones a year. You could earn yourself a lot of money."

Money? Suddenly Raj remembered. Today was Friday, Friday 29th. His last audition. He stood up.

"What time is it?"

"Nearly eight," said Roy.

"Oh no, I've got to be at my last audition at drama school. They'll never believe me if I turn up late."

"They will if a policeman takes you," said one of the police officers. "Where have you got to get to?"

"Central School of Speech and Drama in Swiss Cottage."

"Come on then, we'd better go." Sarah's phone started ringing.

"Hello. Oh, yes, he's here. No, I mean. Look, why don't you speak to him. It's your Mum, Raj."

Raj grabbed the phone. It felt great to hear his mother's voice.

"No, I'm not at Sarah's house. I'm at Blackfriars Police Station. No, I haven't done anything wrong."

The police officer was pointing with his hand at his watch.

"Look, Mum. I've got my last audition now. I've got to go. But I'll be at the Temple tonight. Promise. I'll tell you everything then. I love you."

Raj was saying goodbye to Sarah and her dad on the steps of the police station.

7 **reward** money paid to thank sb if they have found sth or sb – 8 **Metropolitan Police** the police force of Greater London

"I'll take your bike for you, Raj. And next time you need to find your way around London, ask another cabbie." He laughed and walked towards his black cab.

"Thanks, Sarah."

"That's all right. Good luck this morning."

"Thanks. And...."

"Yeah?"

"Thanks for everything." Raj took her hand and gave it a squeeze. He walked towards the police car with the police officer. Then he turned and shouted over his shoulder.

"Think I owe you another meal. Covent Garden again?"

"Sounds good." Sarah laughed. "Now just go and show them what you can really do."

Raj climbed into the front of the police car and the car set off through the streets of Clerkenwell and the City of London. Raj felt really tired but he was ready, ready to take on his next big role.

Think about it...

Do you think Raj will get the part?

What do you think of the title of the book?

If you could chose an alternative, what would it be?

---

2 **cabbie** taxi driver – 9 **squeeze** hold sth tightly – 11 **to owe** to have to pay sb back with sth

Activities

Focus on the story

1. What can you remember?
Tick 👍 *true* or 👎 *false* for the sentences about the story.

👍　👎

a.　Raj's father thinks acting is for fun, not for a job.　☐　☐

b.　Raj goes to the park to look at the city.　☐　☐

c.　Meesha think Raj is their parents' favourite child.　☐　☐

d.　Raj is embarrassed when Sarah criticizes his practise performance.　☐　☐

e.　Raj finds the interview for his new job difficult.　☐　☐

f.　Other actors at the second audition say they have previous acting work.　☐　☐

g.　Raj's mother is very grateful that Raj goes to Neasden Temple.　☐　☐

h.　Ed traps Raj so he feels he has to work for Ed.　☐　☐

2. Finish the sentence
Circle the correct option.

1. Michael and Raj are _____
a. old friends.　　b. at the audition.　　c. related.

2. Raj's uncle is a(n) _____ to Raj.
a. inspiration　　b. bad example　　c. kind relative

3. Raj lives _____ from the centre of London.
a. a quarter of an hour　b. half an hour　　c. three quarters of an hour

4. Raj accuses his father of paying _____ the minimum wage.

a. the same as   b. more than   c. less than

5. The park warden _____ Raj.

a. helps   b. listens to   c. threatens

6. The Knowledge is a test for _____

a. bike couriers.   b. lorry drivers.   c. taxi drivers.

7. In the future, Raj would like to do _____

a. theatre for the radio.   b. present a show on the radio.

c. interviews for the radio.

8. There are _____ spaces available at the Central School of Speech and Drama each year.

a. 3000   b. unlimited   c. 25

9. The scene for one of the other pieces at the audition was_____

a. in a kitchen.   b. on public transport.

c. in a garden.

10. There was a _____ at Neasden temple.

a. birthday celebration   b. special religious service

c. special performance

Focus on grammar

1. Complete the sentences about the story.

   a. The more Lottery tickets Raj's father sells, the _____ (happy) he is.

   b. The _____ Raj insists he wants to be an actor, the angrier his father becomes.

   c. The quicker Raj transports parcels, the _____ money he earns.

   d. The _____ (busy) Raj becomes with work, the more upset Sarah becomes.

   e. The more Raj argues with Ed, _____ angrier Ed becomes.

   f. The more phones Ed's gang steal, the more _____ (likely) they will be caught.

   g. _____ longer Raj waits in Ed's office, the more tired he feels.

   h. The _____ (near) the audition, the more excited and nervous Raj is.

2. Choose the correct answer to complete the dialogue between Raj and Meesha.

Meesha: Raj comes first, our Golden Boy! And is our First-born coming to the temple tonight?
Raj: I'm not a Golden Boy, I'm just the only boy in the family and 1. _____ the only girl.

Meesha: You have always 2. _____ the favourite, father asks you to work in the shop every weekend and wants you to take over the business.

Raj: You work in the shop every Saturday afternoon! Anyway, you're lucky he doesn't want you 3. _____ take over the business. You're free to do what you want.

Meesha: That's not true, they're just not interested in me. Whenever you are studying, I am being 4. _____ to cook in the kitchen. How can I get a good job if I am always cooking instead of studying?

Raj: You do study as well, you can do both. You love maths, you can study that and get a job using your maths – I am being forced to study business, 5. _____ I hate.

Meesha: At least our parents care about you 6. _____ a job, they just want me to be a good housewife in the future.

Raj: You don't have to be a housewife if you 7. _____ want to be.

Meesha: I don't want to be!

Raj: Well then, you can decide what you 8. _____ to do…

Meesha: I want to be a famous mathematician!

1. a. you're	b. your	c. you
2. a. being	b. been	c. be
3. a. (nothing)	b. will	c. to
4. a. made	b. make	c. making
5. a. which	b. who	c. but
6. a. get	b. to get	c. getting
7. a. won't	b. didn't	c. don't
8. a. want	b. will want	c. would want

3. What happened?

Put the pictures from the story in the correct order and write about what happened.

Building your vocabulary

1. Which verb goes with which preposition?

Draw a line to match the verb and prepositions together to complete the phrasal verbs from the story. Then, write a sentence for each one.

a) put	a) over
b) turn	b) for
c) take	c) up to
d) run	d) run
e) get	e) in
f) look	f) off
g) drop	g) on
h) fill	h) off

a. ___I put on my coat before I leave the house in the morning.___

b. _____

c. _____

d. _____

e. _____

f. _____

g. _____

h. _____

2. How is Raj feeling?

Choose the word that best describes how Raj is feeling at these stages of the story.

uncomfortable   intimidated   anxious   hopeful
bored   confident   impatient   determined

a. Page 6, lines 9 – 14 _____

b. Page 8, lines 16 – 17 _____

c. Page 12, lines 10 – 13 _____

d. Page 29, lines 21 – 23 _____

e. Page 22, lines 25 – 29 _____

f. Page 31, lines 19 – 20 _____

g. Page 36, lines 6 – 17 _____

h. Page 40, lines 1 – 4 _____

3. Crossword puzzle

Use the clues to complete the crossword.

Across

1 theatre associated with William Shakespeare
4 a person who trains actors' voices
5 centre of the Indian film industry
6 the area of a theatre where the audience sits
9 a place where people can watch a performance
10 famous play by Shakespeare, set in Verona
11 performance without fixed text or music

Down

2 international theatre festival in Scotland
3 a person who pretends to be someone else while performing in a film or theatre
6 short performance by an actor to prove his/her ability/suitability for a particular play, film or show, or in Raj's case for getting a place at the Central School of Speech and Drama
7 a longer speech made by one actor, alone
8 most famous playwright and poet of the English language

The 6:42 from London Bridge – the mind map

Make your own mind map with words connected to the story.
Think of words to add to each topic area. You can add your own
topic areas too.

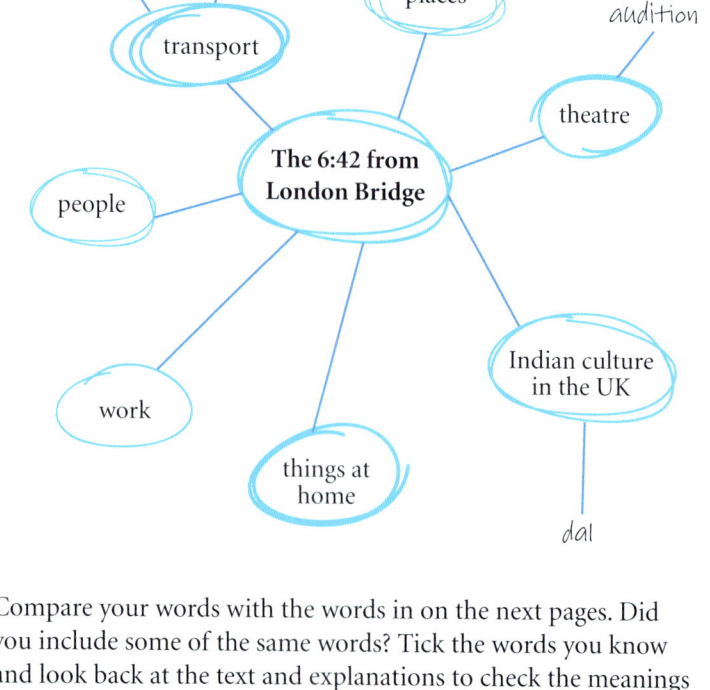

Compare your words with the words in on the next pages. Did
you include some of the same words? Tick the words you know
and look back at the text and explanations to check the meanings
of any new words. You can add your own words and notes to the
glossary like the examples here.

Glossary

	New word?	Notes / connected words
Indian culture in the UK		
Bollywood	☐	
chapatti	☐	
dal	☐	
Diwali	☐	
incense	☐	
lassi	☐	*Indian yoghurt drink*
onion bhaji	☐	
paratha	☐	
samosa	☐	
Places		
auditorium	☐	
compartment	☐	
department store	☐	
dock	☐	
flight of steps	☐	
garage	☐	
phone box	☐	
prayer hall	☐	
temple	☐	
tube station	☐	
warehouse	☐	
People		
boss	☐	
commuter	☐	
crook	☐	
madman	☐	
shopper	☐	
tutor	☐	

	New word?	**Notes / connected words**

Theatre

actor	☐
audition	☐
casting	☐
drama school	☐
improvisation	☐
interval	☐
monologue	☐
recall	☐
role	☐
speech	☐
stage	☐
stalls	☐
voice coach	☐

Things at home

basket	☐
carpet	☐
cigar	☐
envelope	☐
gate	☐
glove	☐
kite	☐
lantern	☐
parcel	☐
supper	☐

Things at home

bike	☐
ferry	☐
helmet	☐
pedestrian	☐
route	☐

	New word?	**Notes / connected words**
Work		
applicant	☐	
business head	☐	
Business Studies	☐	
courier	☐	
insurance	☐	
lorry	☐	
park warden	☐	
print out	☐	
project	☐	
run (the shop)	☐	
Saturday job	☐	
social security number	☐	

Find out more

1. Look at these place names which were mentioned in the story. Try to find where they are on a map of London and group them according to their location. Put N (north), S (south), E (east), W (west) by each one.

Aldwych
Big Ben
Canary Wharf
Covent Garden
The Globe
Greenwich
Hampstead Heath
Leicester Square
London Bridge
London Eye
Millennium Bridge
National Theatre
Neasden Temple / Shree Swaminarayan Mandir
Oxford Street
OXO Tower
Parliament Hill
Portobello Road
Selfridges
South Bank
Southwark
St Paul's Cathedral
Swiss Cottage
The Strand
Tower Bridge
Waterloo Station
Wembley
Willesden

2. How long does it take? Find out how long it takes on each form of transport and decide on the quickest way from:

🚶 from	🚌	🚶	🚊	🚲	to
Covent Garden					Tower Bridge
Selfridges					National Theatre
Southwark					Greenwich
London Eye					The Globe
Canary Wharf					Portobello Road

3. London is a very diverse city. Find 10 interesting facts which show just how diverse the city is:

Answer key

Focus on the story

1. 1. a. true, b. false, c. true, d. true, e. false, f. true, g. true, h. true

2. 1. b   5. a   9. b
    2. a   6. c   10. b
    3. b   7. a
    4. c   8. c

Focus on grammar

1. a. happier, b. more, c. more, d. busier, e. the, f. likely, g. the, h. nearer

2. 7. 1. a, 2. b, 3. c, 4. a, 5. a, 6. c, 7. c, 8. A

3. 2, 6, 9 5, 3, 4, 1, 7, 8

Focus on words and phrases

1. a. put on (coats), b. turn up to (an event/place), c. take over (the shop), d. run off, e. get in, f. look for, g. drop off, h. fill in

2. a. anxious, b. bored, c. determined, d. intimidated, e. confident, f. impatient, g. uncomfortable, h. hopeful

3. Across: 1. The Globe, 4. voice coach, 5. Bollywood, 6. auditorium, 9. Theatre, 10. Romeo and Juliet, 11. Improvisation; Down: 2. Edinburgh Festival, 3. actor, 6. audition, 7. monologue, 8 Shakespeare

The Regent's Park
LISSON GROVE
The Sherlock Holmes Museum
Baker Street
Regent's Park
Great Portland Street
Warren Street
Euston Square
Euston
Edgware Road
Westway
PADDINGTON
Sussex Gardens
Marble Arch
Hyde Park Pl
MARYLEBONE
The British Museum
Tottenham Court Road
Oxford Circus
Bond Street
Hanover Square
SOHO
MAYFAIR
Leicester Square
Piccadilly Circus
National Portrait Gallery
Charing Cross Underground
Green Park
St James's Palace
Hyde Park
The Long Water
The Serpentine
W Carriage Dr
Hyde Park Corner
Constitution Hill
Buckingham Palace
St James's Park
Birdcage Walk
Knightsbridge
St. James's Park
Westminster Abbey
WESTMINSTER
Great Peter St
London Oratory
Victoria and Albert Museum
Victoria
Westminster Cathedral
Horseferry Rd
Sloane Square
Sloane Ave
Cale St
Pimlico
Vauxhall Bridge Rd
Chelsea Bridge Rd
Grosvenor Rd
CHELSEA
Thames
Battersea Park Children's Zoo
Battersea Park
Nine Elms Ln
Battersea Park Rd
Albert Bridge Rd